MW00959824

THE 1619 PROJECT

Table of Contents

Chapter 1

A Seismic Shift

In August of 1619, a pirate ship sailed its way through the still-warm waters of The Atlantic Ocean, heading north along the coast of North America, a continent that was known to most Europeans at the time as the New World.

Indeed, those ruddy pirates would have seen a very different coastline from what one sees today. Today, the Eastern Seaboard is littered with cities, hotels, resorts, condos, and more than a few large industrial buildings, factories, and warehouses that serve a wide variety of modern purposes. But, in 1619, just 12 years after the founding of Jamestown, Virginia, and a year before any Puritans landed at Plymouth Rock, the New World was wild and verdant, stippled with pockets of native fishing villages that would have been so ingeniously blended into their natural surrounding that one would have to be within spear-shot to actually see them.

No, at this time, those pirates would have seen—fitting for the name of the British colony they were approaching—virgin land.

This pirate ship arrived at Jamestown and the British colony of Virginia, carrying an expensive cargo they hoped to sell to the colonists—Africans.

The ship's crew had stolen the Africans, somewhere around 20 or 30 of them, from a Portuguese slave ship. That slave ship had captured the men and women from an area of Africa that would now be part of the country of Angola.

Slaves were indeed expensive cargo. They had to be guarded, which required manpower, or else they could escape their bonds and prove dangerous. They also required a minimum of food and water—precious commodities on the open sea. The longer the slaves stayed aboard, the thinner the profit margin would be, which would have to be split into equal shares for the crew. Needless to say, these pirates were hoping the colonists would find use for the Africans and pay something for them.

It turns out they did.

These 20-30 purchased African slaves proved to be the beginning of slavery in the British colonies, the start of a 250-year culture of slavery in a land that would later become the United States.

The 1619 Project

In August of 2019, on the 400-year anniversary of the above-described introduction of African slavery to the British colonies and America, The New York Times Magazine released a 100-pages spread called The 1619 Project, a collection of essays and profiles that discusses the history and legacy of slavery in the US and, in the words of its authors, "aims to reframe the country's history by placing the consequences of slavery and the contributions of Black Americans at the very center of the United States' national narrative."

While it is true that both slavery and Africans were no strangers to the Americas prior to the story detailed above in 1619, this was the first time African slavery was brought to the British colonies.

The 1619 Project would grow beyond a single magazine special. It would later include a newspaper article, live events, a podcast, a line of books for children and adults, and a school curriculum that school systems across the country have adopted to bring slavery and black history to the fore in their American history classrooms.

A Controversial Project

Within academic circles, the accuracy of many statements within the collected essays was questioned, as was the entire theme of the project in attempting to "reframe American history," casting historical people and events into an entirely different light.

Even as historians weighed in, journalists were doing the same, fact-checking and criticizing, and praising the project for its bold statements and unique perspective. Several magazines and newspapers got involved, including The Wall Street Journal and Politico.

Finally, even politicians got involved. Some thanked The New York Times Magazine for forcing the American public to take an honest look at US history and re-examine some of the long-held stories about the birth and youth of our nation. At the same time, others rallied against the project, saying it was mocking American

Heroes of the American Revolutionary War and The American Civil War.

In May of 2020, Nikole-Hannah-Jones, the lead writer and developer of the project, was awarded the Pulitzer Prize for Commentary for her moving opening essay in the August 2019 issue of The New York Times Magazine. In that essay, opening The 1619 Project, Hannah-Jones described, among other things, the purchase of those first African slaves at Point Comfort from the English privateer, White Lion, who had captured the 20-30 Africans during a series of African-Portuguese raids against the African Kingdom of Ndonga.

In September of 2020, the project came under criticism for retroactively changing some of the facts and wording in the original essays without publishing any editorial notes.

Yes, this project generated a years-long discussion of American heritage, history, and identity. While it is true that many factual and ideological criticisms found footing and prompted corrections to the project, even many of the staunchest critics of the project also admitted that this was a conversation that needed to be had.

The Project that Generates New Conversations

The 1619 Project was not just a single issue of The New York Times Magazine. An ongoing regular series in that magazine and other Times publications, including the newspaper, added articles and essays to the national conversation.

In addition to this, the Pulitzer Center and the Smithsonian got involved, recruiting historians, journalists, and academics to help fact-check the project, add to it, and design companion materials.

Among these materials are classroom worksheets and lesson plans, available for free on the Pulitzer Center's website for schools across the nation to include in their history classes. The project also grew into a book of the same name (1619), other spin-off books for kids and adults, and a podcast from The Daily, the morning news podcast of the Times.

This far-reaching project has started up several fascinating (and occasionally heated) conversations at a national level.

For example, The 1619 Project asserts that, because of the massive influence of African slavery and Black Americans on American history, 1619 should be considered the birth year of our nation instead of the traditional 1776. This idea brought about a great deal of criticism and argument from all political and ideological sides.

In addition to that, The 1619 Project cites slavery as a major motivation for American Independence, claiming that the colonists' reluctance to give up slavery caused them to start the American Revolutionary War in the first place. After criticism, The New York Times Magazine walked back this statement slightly, but the resulting discussion has caused many to rethink the US's cultural (if not political) origins.

The 1619 Project traces African Slavery as a major influence in American culture and society, from music to the prison system to American sports. Many of these connections have been applauded by activists and academics, while others view these connections as a stretch at best and a downright re-writing of history to fit ideological concepts at worst.

Speaking of re-writing history, is this what The 1619 Project is trying to do? Does US history need re-writing, perhaps, as a means to re-contextualize some of our nation's most deeply-held myths and stories? When one goes back and plays with the facts of history, are they restoring it or ruining it?

Indeed, The 1619 Project forces all Americans to rethink what they believe they know about their own nation. For many, this new take on history rights a wrong. For others, it distorts the facts and turns once-believed American heroes into "white supremacists."

But what exactly did the original magazine special include, and what made it so controversial?

Chapter 2

The 1619 Project

The August 14, 2019 issue of The New York Times Magazine was dedicated entirely to The 1619 Project (with the exception of the crossword sudoku puzzles in the back), making the project's initial length a mere 100 pages. However, those 100 pages started a kind of journalistic revolution, sparking a fresh conversation on race, history, systemic corruption, ideology, and what it means to be American.

But what did this original issue of The New York Times Magazine include? What essays would go on to spark so much conversation and controversy?

The Opening Essay by Nikole Hannah-Jones

The opening piece of The 1619 Project was possibly the most controversial, an essay by Nikole Hannah-Jones entitled "America Wasn't a

Democracy Until Black American's Made It One."
This is the essay that won the Pulitzer Prize for
Commentary in 2020.

This opening essay had two major purposes:
First, it set the theme and tone for the entire
project to come, opening with a description of
the pirate ship (actually an English privateer
ship) selling the first black slaves to a British
colony in 1619, giving the reasoning behind the
title of the project. Second, the essay followed
the narrative explained in its name that Black
Americans essentially made the American
Democracy we know today.

That second concept, which is spelled out in the
title of the opening essay, is intriguing and
backed up by facts, connections, anecdotes, and
opinions.

Small details add to the argument, such as the
fact that the first person to die for American
independence was a black man, Crispus
Attucks, a fugitive of slavery himself. "In every
war this nation has waged since that first one,"
Hannah-Jones writes, "black Americans have
fought." She then points out that African
Americans are most likely to join the US military
of all other racial groups.

Her point stretches beyond black Americans serving in the military, however. She argues that the principles set up in the Declaration of Independence were essentially falsified by a nation that continued to embrace slavery. It was not until continual resistance, and fighting for civil rights did black Americans create the land of freedom the founding fathers wrote about.

The opening words, if not the document in its entirety, of the Declaration of Independence, are taught to students across the country. "We hold these truths to be self-evident, that all men are created equal, that they are endowed by their Creator with certain unalienable rights, that among these are Life, Liberty, and the pursuit of Happiness."

Hannah-Jones points out that, when Thomas Jefferson wrote those words, a young black man was standing nearby, a slave Jefferson owned, ready to obey whatever order Jefferson gave. The land of freedom and equality Jefferson imagined obviously did not include people of color - yet.

However, that opening essay did much more than point out that America was not the land of freedom it aspired to be for many generations. It also looks at historical events and people through the lens of slavery, painting some of America's most-loved stories and heroes in an unsavory light.

American colonists called themselves slaves of Britain, demanding their freedom, which, Hannah-Jones points out, was an irony Britain did not miss. English writer Samuel Johnson wrote, "How is it that we hear the loudest yelps liberty among the drivers of slaves?"

Nevertheless, Hannah-Jones takes it even further. She writes: "It is not incidental that 10 of the nation's first 12 presidents were enslavers, and some might argue that this nation was founded not as a democracy but as a slavocracy."

In the original version of the essay, which has since been edited to "soften" the message, it was also suggested that the American Revolution happened in the first place precisely because Britain was starting to abolish slavery, and this was a threat to most colonists' livelihood. Essentially, the argument goes, Americans fought for independence to defend their right to own slaves.

Chained Migration: How Slavery Made Its Way West

This essay, by Tiya Miles, a professor at the history department at Harvard, chronicles the march of slavery west during the early 1800s. The main argument of her contribution is that it was slavery that allowed white Americans to seek out more and more land, forcibly displacing Native American populations in order to procure said lands.

In other words, white American capitalists sought out more land for their plantations precisely because the slave system would allow them to work for larger fields than they could ever work themselves (or pay someone a fair wage for).

In keeping with the tradition already established in The 1619 Project, Miles did not mince words, even when speaking about historical events and people. "President Andrew Jackson," she wrote, "an enslaver from Tennessee famous for brutal 'Indian' fighting in Georgia and Florida, swooped in on the side of fellow enslavers, championing the Indian Removal Act of 1830." That act would result in the expulsion of man native peoples from their ancestral land.

Meanwhile, as slave labor extended far beyond the regions of the original 13 colonies, as Miles puts it, "white enslavers back east realized that their most profitable export was no longer tobacco or rice. A complex interstate slave trade became an industry of its own."

Miles also provides some new context to an established historical event—the Mexican-American War:

"Armed conflict between American-identified enslavers and a Mexican state that outlawed slavery in 1829 was among the causes of the Mexican-American War, which won for the United States much of the Southwest and California."

Miles's essay continues into more modern times, pointing out the fight that black Americans fought to bring freedom and equality to the country they both loved and were oppressed by. "No one cherishes freedom more than those who have not had it," she writes. "And to this day, black Americans, more than any other group, embrace the democratic ideals of a common good."

Other Essays of Note

Mathew Desmond, a professor of sociology at Princeton University, wrote a striking piece called "American Capitalism is Brutal. You Can Trace That to the Plantation." He traces the brutality against slaves in the plantation system to the exploitative practices of the modern workplace, including treating many workers much like cattle, even installing software on company computers to count employees' keystrokes and mouse clicks as a way of micro-managing them.

Desmond labels modern capitalism as cruel and barbaric. The full-page caption on page 31 says, "In order to understand the brutality of American capitalism, you have to start on the plantation."

A short piece of the cotton trade pointed out that the international textile market paved the way for modern global corporate deals and trade agreements. This was written by Mehrsa Baradaran, a professor at U.C. Irvine School of Law.

Tiya Miles, who authored one of the essays mentioned above, also wrote "How Slavery Built Wall Street," a fascinating look at the origins of the modern center for American commerce. Miles writes, "It is uncanny, but perhaps predictable, that the original wall for which Wall Street is named was built by the enslaved at a site that served as the city's first organized slave auction."

Even after slavery was abolished in the northern states, such as New York, the businessmen of Wall Street continued to profit from the ownership and exploitation of people by investing heavily in southern plantations, which, of course, used slaves.

Later essays trace various other aspects of modern American society to slavery and race issues, including healthcare (in Jeneen Interlandi's "Why Doesn't America Have Universal Healthcare? One Word: Race"), music (in Wesley Morris's "Why is Everyone Always Stealing Black Music?"), medicine (in Linda Villarosa's "How False Beliefs in Physical Racial Differences Still Live in Medicine Today"), prisons (in Bryan Stevenson's "Why American Prisons owe Their Cruelty to Slavery") and even traffic jams in major cities (in Kevin Kruse's "How Segregation Caused Your Traffic Jam").

Photography and Poetry
In addition to the essays, which make up the meat of the issue's content, The 1619 Project

also contains numerous photos and illustrations. In fact, the issue ends with a photo essay entitled "Their Ancestors Were Enslaved by Law. Now They're Lawyers," a multi-page feature that includes photos by Djeneba Aduayom and text captions by Nikole Hannah-Jones and Wadzanai Mhute.

Photos include images of slaves working in plantations, black American activists standing up for civil justice, the poor and downtrodden suffering from various aspects of modern societal injustice, and historical paintings of slaves and black Americans as part of various aspects of United States history.

Another recurring feature throughout the issue is the running collection of poems and stories, pieces short enough to fit on a single page or less.

The Overall Theme of the Project

As one can see from the overview, The 1619 Project exposed details and made claims that would change the way many thought about American history and culture.

The project's overall theme is this: slavery is a topic that is not discussed enough in schools and history books. Slavery, segregation, and black Americans have shaped the culture of US so significantly that 1619 could be established at the birth year of our nation instead of 1776.

According to this project, nearly every aspect of our culture, government, economy, and identity grows directly or indirectly from our history of enslavement.

However, how would the world react to such claims?

Chapter 3

Making Waves

Without a doubt, The 1619 Project ruffled some feathers, forcing people of all races to see their nation, their history, and their race in a slightly different light.

Some applauded this fresh look at US history, saying it helps correct a narrative that likes to ignore the ugly facts regarding slavery and segregation. On the other hand, others have criticized The New York Times Magazine for playing fast and loose with historical facts, ignoring esteemed historians and scholars, and inserting ideologies and identity into history.

The creators of the project knew their essays, poems, and photographs would rock some boats. Trymaine Lee, one of the contributors to the project, a Pulitzer Prize winner, as well as an Emmy Award-winning correspondent for MSNBC, said, "I think there will be some discomfort in the idea of that reflection that you see back may not be as pretty as the picture you've been given your entire life." He continues, "But for many people of us who have contributed to the project, we are black people in America who have lived this, whose families have lived this."

So what has the response been for The 1619 Project, the good, the bad, and the ugly?

Praise for the Project
Nikole Hannah-Jones, one of the principal contributors to the project, was awarded the Pulitzer Prize for Commentary in 2020 for her opening essay in the project. That in itself is great praise for the journalistic work. But many others have piped in with their own commendation.

Manisha Sinha, a professor of history at the University of Connecticut and a leading authority on the history of slavery and abolition, would later be asked to contribute to the ongoing version of The 1619 Project. Before that, however, she looked at the original magazine version of the project as an outsider. While she admitted that there were some minor inaccuracies in the essays and that the critiques some were making provided an opportunity for one to "engage in discussion with." Talking about the August 2019 issue of the Times, she said, "It was a worthy thing to actually shine a light on a subject that the average person on the street doesn't know much about."

Nell Irvin Painter, a professor emeritus of history at Princeton, said, "I support The 1619 Project as kind of a cultural event."

Even the most vigorous opponents of the project admitted that what The New York Times Magazine was doing had great merit, it being a discussion that needed to happen. In one letter, a group of acclaimed historians argued against the accuracy and legitimacy of various aspects of the project. Even so, that same letter, sent to the Times, says, "We applaud all efforts to address the foundational centrality of slavery and racism to our history."

It stands to reason that a nation whose economy and way of life depended on slavery for hundreds of years would be shaped by that same slavery in one way or another. Moreover, the racism and segregation that continued long after the abolition of slavery would still shape many aspects of our society for generations.

And yet, as the contributors of the project have worked hard to point out, the issues of slavery and racism are usually dismissed. American heroes of history, our founding fathers, the ones that shaped our history and laws, were also manly slave-owners themselves. This is not something mentioned in school history books nearly as much as it should be.

Leslie M. Harris, writing for Politico, another critic of the project, had this to say, "Overall, The 1619 Project is a much-needed corrective to the blindly celebratory histories that once dominated our understanding of the past—histories that wrongly suggested racism and slavery were not a central part of US history."

Wilentz, another critic of the project, wrote, "All of us think that the idea of The 1619 Project is fantastic. I mean, it's just urgently needed. The idea of bringing to light not only scholarship but all sorts of things that have to do with the centrality of slavery and of racism to American history is a wonderful idea."

Perhaps the highest possible praise a project like this can receive is in how many people found themselves reading and discussing it. Ideally, the purpose of the magazine issue was not to denounce white Americans or spark a revolution. Instead, it was to spark difficult conversations that could teach future generations a better way.

"They had not seen this type of demand for a print product of The New York Times, they said, since 2008, when people wanted copies of Obama's historic presidency edition," Hannah-Jones said. Yes, the August 2019 issue of Times was one of the highest-selling ever. Hannah-Jones continues, "I know when I talk to people, they have said they feel they are understanding the architecture of their country in a way that they had not."

Of course, as powerful as the positive reception of the project was, the negative response was just as great and probably a bit more vocal.

Historians Push Back
Within months of the magazine's original publication, historians and scholars started questioning some of the project's facts and ideas. One such historian was Sean Wilentz, mentioned above. The Princeton historian called the project cynical in a lecture in November. He would go on to do much more about the issue.

After the November lecture, Wilentz began circulating a letter that objected to the project. He managed to get four other historians to sign the letter before sending it directly to the Times. Those historians were James McPherson, Gordon Wood, Victoria Bynum, and James Oaks. Each of the signatories are top scholars in their field.

According to the letter, which would later be published in the Times, The 1619 Project was "a displacement of historical understanding by ideology." These scholars both disagreed with the project and demanded that certain corrections be made.

Even so, the goal of these historians was not to somehow disqualify the project. Instead, as Wilentz would later say in an interview: "Far from an attempt to discredit The 1619 Project, our letter is intended to help it."

This idea of wanting to improve the project was not uncommon. In fact, some journalists and scholars who had spoken out against the project would later be asked to contribute to it. Moreover, indeed, the project did respond to critiques. Jake Silverstein, the editor of The New York Times Magazine, published a detailed rebuttal to the letter Wilentz and other had signed. And yet, many minor changes were made to the project in later printings. The criticism did improve the project.

Some of the scholars against the project were not as constructive. They were instead opting to question the very premise of the project and throw stones at the Time for its lack of journalistic and scholarly integrity.

Gordon Wood, one of the scholars that signed Wilentz's letter, a Pulitzer Prize-winning historian of the American Revolution, said The 1619 Project was "so wrong in so many ways."

Another signatory of the letter was James McPherson. He is dean of Civil War historians and another possessor of a Pulitzer Prize. He said the project was an "unbalanced, one-sided account." He continued, "[it] left most of the history out."

It is essential to keep in mind that the scholars in question are not towing a political line. As we will see in a future section, politics did come into play as a response to this project, but the historians and scholars that objected to the August issue of The New York Times Magazine were not doing so as for political motivations. In fact, Wood and McPherson are generally considered liberal historians, and their original interviews appeared on "socialist" websites. So no, this was not a conservative ploy. Instead, this was about scholars that took professional issues with the project and wanted to correct it.

James Oaks, referring to the ideological slant the project put on history, said, "The worst thing about it is that it leads to political paralysis." In other words, The 1619 Project is shocking and controversial, but it is not helpful at all.

Internationally regarded historians were not the only ones that pushed back against The 1619 Project, however. As we will see in the following section, there was also quite a critique that stemmed from the journalistic world.

The Journalism of the Project is Questioned

While some took issue with the historical significance of claims made in The 1619 Project, others were more worried about the fact-checking, accuracy, and journalistic integrity of many of the projects' essays. While many journals praised the project and Times for shining a much-needed light on slavery in US history, several have also shared concerns about the accuracy and journalistic integrity of the project.

Leslie M. Harris is a professor of history at Northwestern University. In a Politico article, she wrote called "I Helped Fact-Check The 1619 Project. The Times Ignored Me" Harris writes these opening words: "On August 19 of last year [2019] I listened in stunned silence as Nikole Hannah-Jones, a reporter for The New York Times Magazine, repeated an idea that I had vigorously argued against with her fact-checker."

According to Harris, an editor for the magazine reached out to her with some points from the project. Harris took issue with the idea that the American Revolution was basically an attempt to keep slavery going. She cited facts that proved this not to be the case, and the editor even came back with questions for clarification, although the follow-up questions did not seem to relate directly to Harris's primary issue with the project.

"Despite my advice," Harris writes, "the Time published the incorrect statement about the American Revolution anyway, in Hannah-Jones' introductory essay."

The fact that the Times did not dive deeper into the issues after fact-checkers got back dissenting views from leading authorities is shocking, if nothing else, based on Hannah-Jones's own statement about another critique of the project mentioned above. When Hannah-Jones was asked about the letter Welintz and other scholars sent to the Times, she explicitly stated that they would have taken their views very seriously had the letter come before the magazine came out. She went on to criticize those historians for waiting until the magazine was out to start discrediting it.

Hannah-Jones's point is a fair one. However, her claim that they would have taken those historians seriously is eroded by what Harris writes, someone that offered a critique beforehand-and a critique backed up with academic fact—and yet she was ignored.

"The paper's characterizations of slavery in America reflected laws and practices more common in the antebellum era than in Colonial Times, and did not accurately illustrate the varied experiences of the first generation of enslaved people that arrived in Virginia in 1619," Harris writes.

"political (originally communist) propaganda, esp. in art or literature"

Harris was not the only one to question journalism behind the project, and neither was Politico. Damon Linker, writing in The Week, said the project presented history "in a highly sensationalistic, reductionistic, and tendentious way, with the cumulative result resembling agitprop more than responsible journalism or scholarship."

1937

"Guernica

Pablo

Picasso

Other publications that presented a similar attitude include the National Review, New York, and Bloggingheads.tv.

Writing for The Atlantic, Adam Serwer wrote in an article entitled "The Fight Over The 1619 Project is Not About the Facts" about how the project is pessimistic in nature. He said, "The most radical threat in The 1619 Project is not its contention that slavery's legacy continues to shape American institutions; it's the authors' pessimism that a majority of white people will abandon racism and work with black Americans toward a more perfect union."

According to Serwer, just about every essay in the project talks about racial prejudice as having to be continually endured. "It is this profound pessimism about white America that many of The 1619 Project's critics find most galling."

Writing for City Journal, Allen Guelzo called the project a "conspiracy theory." He adds, "In no human society has an enslaved people suddenly found itself vaulted into positions of such privilege, and with the consent—even the approbation—of those who were once the enslavers."

Erick Erickson, a conservative pundit, went so far as to call the project a Neo-Confederate worldview. This view says, as he put it, that the "South actually won the Civil War by weaving itself into the fabric of post-war society so it can then discredit the entire American enterprise."

Certainly, journalists and journals alike have had their criticisms of The 1619 Project. The backlash, however, goes so far as to reach the political spectrum.

The 1619 Project Affects Politics in Surprising Ways

Political figures were affected in various ways by the claims made in the project. Democratic Senator Kamala Harris praised the magazine and the project, saying it "is a powerful and necessary reckoning of our history." She would go on to say, "We cannot understand and address the problems of today without speaking truth about how we got here."

Newt Gingrich, former Speaker of the United States House of Representatives, called the project "brainwashing propaganda." He noted that "there were several hundred thousand white Americans who died in the Civil War in order to free the slaves."

President Donald Trump told Chris Wallace in an interview on Fox News the following: "I just look at—I look at school. I watch, I read, look at the stuff. Now they want to change—1492, Columbus discovered America. You know, we grew up, we all did, that's what we learned. Now they want to make it The 1619 Project. Where did that come from? What does it represent? I don't even know."

In fact, some politicians decided to do more than just talk about what they did not like about the project. Some decided to take legislative actions. Republican Senator Tom Cotton of Arkansas proposed the "Saving American History Act" in July of 2020. This act would penalize public schools that included educational materials like those related to The 1619 Project by denying them federal funding. Later, when President

Trump heard that California schools were including the project in their classrooms, he said he would investigate it and pull federal funding.

In November of 2020, Trump established the 1776 Commission through an executive order. This commission was tasked with creating a written response to The 1619 Project. This document was created and published in January of 2021, although it was immediately criticized for poor scholarliness and a lack of academic rigor. As a result, president Biden pulled the plug on the Project on January 20, 2021.

The fact that a government-sponsored response to The 1619 Project was unable to meet even the most basic academic and journalistic standard illustrates something about the original 1619 Project—that creating such an extensive collection of written works and holding them to a high standard is a difficult thing. While the editors and contributors to the Times project are leading journalists and scholars, the masterful work they produced still included some errors and extreme statements that had to be walked back later.

Perhaps the high-quality journalism of The 1619 Project could not be fully appreciated until someone tried to replicate it for the opposing view.

Furthering the Conversation

The prime objective of The 1619 Project was not to re-educate all of America. It was not to "set the record straight" or re-write history. Instead, the project's main objective was to spark conversation, get people talking—and questioning—US history and the part slavery played in our history and culture for centuries.

Despite the scholarly, journalistic, and even political backlash the project instigated, the goal was achieved with that objective in mind. For the first time in decades, perhaps since the height of the Civil Rights movement, mainstream America had to take a long, hard look at our culture and history and the influences slavery and racial injustice have had on America.

Adam Serwer writes, "Both sides agree... that slavery's legacy still shapes American life." That concept is more widely known than ever before, and that is thanks to The 1619 Project.

On the other hand, the critics have succeeded in one sense, in that the public eye has been distracted from the most prominent issues.

Leslie M. Harris writes, "I was concerned that the critics would use the overstated claim [that the slavery was a main motivation for the American Revolution] to discredit the entire undertaking. So far, that's exactly what has happened."

Before we get deeper into the impact 1619 has had, let us analyze two of the controversial statements the project has had, starting with the year in the title. Should 1619 be considered the birth year of America?

Chapter 4

When Was America Born?

We were all taught in school that the United States' birth date is July 4, 1776. This is the date of the signing of the Declaration of Independence, not when the war for independence was won, not when the constitution was ratified, nor when the first of the British colonies were founded, nor when Columbus discovered the New World.

Why was this date chosen, the date we commemorate every Fourth of July? And why does The 1619 Project suggest the possibility of changing that date, of retroactively shifting the birth year of our nation to the day black slaves arrived in the colony of Virginia?

What response has there been for this concept? What have historians and journalists had to say about it?

1776—What we Were Taught in School

The 1619 Project asks readers to consider "what it would mean to regard 1619 as our nation's birth year." However, before we can do that, let us take a moment to consider what we are all taught in school.

Why is 1776 set as the birth year of our nation? The signing of the Declaration of Independence has been embraced as a moment to commemorate because of the ideals outlined in that document, ideals that have continued to form our culture for centuries.

As Conor Friedersdorf, writing for The Atlantic, puts it, "America's original revolutionaries, along with Abraham Lincoln, Frederick Douglas, and Martin Luther King Jr., all placed the universalist ideal of the Declaration of Independence at the center of this country's founding."

Yes, the Declaration of Independence has culturally set the tone for our nation. Many scholars and historians have fought, then, for 1776 and the signing of that document to continue to be taught in schools as the birth year of our nation. With, as Friedersdorf puts it, "the declaration of those revolutionary ideals," as the country's birth year, those very ideals are exalted and remembered.

Friedersdorf continues, "The words put forth in 1776 would inspire people all over the world to insist that governments are meant to secure rights, and that 'when any government becomes destructive of those ends, it is the Right of the People to alter or abolish it.' "

Why then does The 1619 Project ask us to consider a different year?

1619—the Times' Proposal

A central theme of The 1619 Project is that slavery, racism, segregation, and black Americans have significantly shaped almost every aspect of American culture. Everything from our economy and global trading network to our sports, music, prisons, and traffic issues lead back—in one way or another—to the treatment of black Americans.

More than that, as Hannah-Jones points out in her opening essay, black Americans have fought over the generations to make America better, to bring about the democracy that Thomas Jefferson aspired to in his declaration. Much of what she has to say cannot be argued against with facts.

For these reasons, the project asks us to understand 1619 as the true founding of this country, therefore "placing the consequences of slavery and the contributions of black Americans at the very center of the story we tell ourselves about who we are."

In other words, if the interaction of black and white Americans has been the backbone of our cultural heritage, why would the moment that interaction begins be considered the cultural birth of America?

A major critique of this concept says that it keeps the lines between black and white Americans strong, causing us to think in terms of cultural identity. But, as Friedersdorfpoints out, "one might counter that a founding narrative of black subjugation and white oppression needn't be divisive or exclusionary—that everyone born in 2020 is a distinct person from Americans of bygone generations of the same race, that people of any skin color can and should identify with the enslaved victims of 1619 to 1865."

In other words, a modern white American does not have to feel any special kinship with white slave owners, and modern black Americans do not have to feel any special kinship with slaves of generations past. Instead, all Americans can feel a kinship with all past Americans, black or white, or other races. Taking a hard look at slavery does not have to be about throwing blame against any modern person or group of people. Instead, it can be about looking at why things are the way they are, how far we have come, and how much farther we still need to go as a nation to more fully fulfill the ideals in the Declaration of Independence.

While this radical concept put forth in The 1619 Project has been talked about before, this particular project elicited a great deal of discussion about the merits of 1776 vs. 1619 as the birth year of our nation. What response did this particular assertion of the project get?

The Response to the 1619 Concept

Several historians and journalists spoke out against the idea of revising America's birth year from 1776 to 1619. Why? What would happen if such a change were made?

Conor Friedersdorf, quoted above, says this, "I think a revision of the nation's founding date would be a substantive mistake that would impede social justice, diminishing a moment that elicits this country's best while pushing tens of millions of Americans further toward the margins of our national story." What did he mean by that?

Let us look at two aspects of the above quote one at a time. First, how would revising the nation's birth year from 1776 to 1619 in any way impede social justice? Certainly, those that suggest this change believe it would aid in social justice, bringing to the forefront the ongoing effects of slavery on our nation. How could that be detrimental?

Consider this: Would a heavier emphasis on this date bring black and white Americans closer together or farther apart? Would it represent a nation eager to put racial differences behind it or a culture that is contented with spotlighting it for countless generations to come?

In addition to that, many socialist movements today are working to bring justice to the lower working classes, no matter their race. Would focusing on only black American issues take away the power of such movements to help the working poor across the country, be they black, white, or of some other racial background?

As a bonus point from the above quote, Friedersdorf said that changing the commemorated birth year of the US would diminish "a moment that elicits this country's best." In other words, by taking the focus away from 1776, we would be robbing attention from the momentous ideals recorded in the declaration of Independence.

Finally, the above quote also said that this revision would push "tens of millions of Americans further toward the margins of our national story. What is meant by this?

Friedersdorf explains further, saying, "The core reframing that The 1619 Project advocates would unwittingly set back, rather than advance, the causes of equity and racial inclusion. Placing America's founding moment in 1776 honors the diversity of its people in a way that 1619 does not."

In other words, how is this date, 1619, supposed to affect native Americans? What about recent immigrants? What about members of the LGBTQ+ community?

1619, as a year, painted the country neatly in the two shades of black and white, while, in reality, modern America (and, indeed, America at any point in its history, if we are being honest) is much more complex than that.

The year 1776, on the other hand, reveals ideals that apply to any group. Even a family of immigrants that arrive in this country as refugees this year and may one day apply for citizenship will benefit from the Declaration of Independence because that document is a manual for how a citizen should act within a nation. It holds the US, and all its people, to a specific standard, a set of ideals that our nation continues to work and fight to uphold.

While the issue of 1619 vs. 1776 is a scholarly and educational one, there was another claim in the project that was even more incendiary. That claim, involving the American Revolutionary War, will be discussed in the following chapter.

Chapter 5

American Independence

"This argument is explosive."

"It doesn't do justice to history."

"It's brainwashing propaganda."

Those are comments made by historians, journalists, and politicians—all in response to The1619 Project's claim that the American Revolution was largely motivated by a desire to continue the legacy of slavery already present in colonial America.

But why does The New York Times Magazine make this claim? What arguments are there to support it? And what historical facts are working against it? To begin with, let us give attention to the project itself in explaining this "explosive" position.

1619 Project's Claim

The claim in question is found right at the start of The 1619 Project, with Hannah-Jones's opening essay. While lauding the contributions of black Americans in an effort to make American a full democracy, she adds that "one of the primary reasons the colonists decided to declare their independence from Britain was because they wanted to protect the institution of slavery."

This institution, Hannah-Jones claims, produced "tremendous wealth" for white colonists.

She continues, "At the time there were growing calls to abolish slavery throughout the British Empire, which would have badly damaged the economics of colonies in both North and South."

Therefore, the claim goes, when colonists got word that Britain was seriously considering outlawing slavery, they decided they would need their freedom to protect their slavery-fueled economic system.

The argument appears sound when one reads the project itself. Throughout the following essays and contributions, it is made painstakingly clear that slavery worked its way into influencing almost every aspect of American life and culture. Without slaves, the project as a whole says, we would not have the America we have today. The dominating of black slaves and, later, free black Americans, and the fight for freedom and equality those black Americans have answered with, have fundamentally shaped our nation.

Even when a great deal of pushback came from abundant sources, Hannah-Jones did not back down from that claim. On the contrary, she told reporters for The Atlantic, "I do still back up that claim."

"I think someone reading that would assume that this was the case: all 13 colonies and most people involved," she continued. "And I accept that criticism, for sure, but I stand by the claim." She went on to explain that, perhaps, the context for the claim was not clear enough, which is something Time will rectify with future 1619-related materials.

Even historians, such as Manisha Sinha, a leading authority in this era of American history does not fully support the claim Hannah-Jones made to back it up to an extent.

"I do not agree that the American Revolution was just a slaveholders' revolt," she said. "But also understand that the original Constitution did give some ironclad protections to slavery without mentioning it."

Far stronger criticisms were on the way, however.

Historians Fight Back

Leslie M. Harris, the historian and journalist that wrote the Politico article "I Helped Fact-Check The 1619 Project. The Times Ignored Me", was focused entirely on this particular claim regarding the motivations of those that fought in the American Revolution. She wrote: "I vigorously disputed the claim... although slavery was certainly an issue in the American Revolution, the protection of slavery was not one of the main reasons the 13 colonies went to war."

"To teach children that the American Revolution was fought in part to secure slavery," Wilentz said, "would be giving a fundamental misunderstanding not only of what the American Revolution was all about but what America stood for and has stood for since the Founding."

To give some context, Wilentz points out that anti-slavery ideology was something new in the world at that time. It was popping up everywhere, too, not just in Britain. Wilentz pointed out, "There was more anti-slavery activity in the colonies than in Britain."

Adam Serwer agrees, writing in The Atlantic, "Although some southern slave owners likely were fighting the British to preserve slavery, the Revolution was kindled in New England, where prewar anti-slavery sentiment was strongest. Early patriots like James Otis, Jon Adams, and Thomas Paine were opposed to slavery, and the Revolution helped fuel abolitionism in the North."

Adding to that, Harris points out that the northern colonies were already moving towards abolition. It was a gradual process, but it was happening. "Most Northern enslavers freed slaves ahead of the time mandated by law."

The situation, then, just before the Revolution, was not so clear-cut. White southern slave owners no-doubt wanted to preserve their very successful and cruel business models, and so did many northern businessmen that invested heavily in southern plantations. But, overall, the sentiments among northerners regarding slavery were much more conflicted.

Harris puts another nail in the coffin of this claim, saying, "Slavery in the Colonies faced no immediate threat from Great Britain, so colonists wouldn't have needed to secede to protect it. It's true that in 1772, the famous Somerset case ended slavery in England and Wales, but it had no impact on Britain's Caribbean colonies, where the vast majority of black people enslaved by the British labored and died, or in the North American Colonies."

In fact, some 60 years later, when slavery was finally ended in the Caribbean colonies, that was only because of a massive slave revolt. A series of slave rebellions made keeping slaves too expensive an endeavor, so slavery was abolished in the Caribbean then.

Indeed, Hannah-Jones's claim in The 1619 Project does not seem to be backed up by fact. And yet, there may still be some merit to that claim entering the American consciousness. Why?

In Defense of a Factually Poor Claim

While it is wildly erroneous to say the main motivation (or even one of the main motivations) for the Declaration of Independence and the American Revolutionary War was to protect slavery and the rights of slaveholders, that claim may still have some merit as a thought the American public should chew on. Why is that?

As part of the response to the project in general, many have written into the Times to say that they did not know slavery was an issue so far back in American history. Many did not know that several of the founding fathers and early presidents were owners of slaves themselves, including the man that wrote the Declaration of Independence.

Many did not realize that the original US constitution protected slavery without ever mentioning it by name. Nor did the average person recognize that the constitution had to be altered or amended to free slaves or give black Americans certain rights.

Many heroes of American history have been white-washed in a sense, cast in this glow of saintliness. However, to hear that Thomas Jefferson or, many years later, Abraham Lincoln said things about black people that we would consider highly offensive today is a much-needed reminder that history is dirty and ugly. It also reminds us of how far we have come and how far we still need to go.

To realize that even a tiny percentage of the "heroic patriots" that fought and died in the American Revolution may have been doing so to protect their way of life as slaveholders is something all modern Americans need to come to terms with. Hannah-Jones may have over-emphasized this point, but sometimes overemphasizing something is the only way you make sure the point is heard.

Another way to make your point heard is to reach the next generation but getting your ideas and facts out to kids that are just now learning about American history for the first time. The Times has been doing this by providing educational supplements to schools across the country.

Chapter 6

The 1619 Curriculum

Shortly after the tremendous success of the original 1619 Project, plans were made to expand the concept into a series of books and a school curriculum.

But what issues might someone take with the way American history is taught in schools today? Does The 1619 Project fill a need in this regard? And how have students and teachers reacted to this project being taught in schools?

The Holes in History Class

Teachers and school district administrators have a constant struggle. While balancing a budget is often not enough, they must constantly juggle what parents want, what they perceive that students need, and constantly shifting requirements that come down from the state and federal level.

Our public-school teachers work long hours for unfair pay, and they often do so without any community recognition or appreciation. The education system is constantly working to improve, doing what it can with the dollars it has.

That said, when it comes to American history, there are some glaring holes in what students are taught. As Adam Serwer puts it, "Most Americans still learn very little about the lives of the enslaved, or how the struggle over slavery shaped a young nation."

Yes, slavery is taught in schools. Students learn about the American Civil War and the Underground Railroad. However, as Serwer puts it, "few American high-school students know that slavery was the cause of the Civil War, that the Constitution protected slavery without explicitly mentioning it, or that ending slavery required a constitutional amendment." In other words, students are not taught enough about how involved slavery was in our history.

"It's ugly," Nikita Stewart wrote in an article in The New York Times called "Why Can't We Teach This?". "For generations, we've been unwilling to do it."

I knew this!

Stewart challenges schools and teachers in this way: "Think about what it would mean for our education system to properly teach students—young children and teenagers—about enslavement, what they would have to learn about our country." This is the gap The 1619 Project aims to close. The aim is to help students understand the full impact of slavery on history.

Some politicians, teachers, and even parents took issue with the concepts of 1619 being taught in schools. But Jake Silverstein, editor of the Times, says this: "I think that there is a misunderstanding that this curriculum is meant to replace all of US history. It's being used as supplementary material for teaching American history."

What does this supplement include, though?

Features of the Curriculum

In addition to a special "teaching version" of the magazine issue, the Times and the Pulitzer Center have come together to create a plethora of supporting materials for teachers to use as discussion aids in their classrooms. Each lesson plan is free to download from the Pulitzer Center's website. They include discussion guides, worksheets, and readers. Each lesson is designed in such a way that it can be implemented for elementary students up to high school.

Lessons include a reading and listening guide to the original project, a flashcard set of important terms and events, as well as topics like "The Idea of America," based on Hannah-Jones's introductory essay.

Another lesson, entitled "Exploring the Legacy of Slavery in Mass Incarnation," traces the legacy of slavery in the contemporary criminal justice system. Virtually every major essay in the original project has some additional material available to foster student discussion and reflection, inviting them to engage with the ideas in the curriculum in, as the Pulitzer Center puts it, "creative and challenging ways."

Teachers and Students React

In a previous chapter, we saw how some politicians reacted very negatively to the idea of teaching The 1619 Project in schools. Then-president Trump, for example, threatened to pull federal funding from any state that allowed this curriculum into its schools. How have teachers and students reacted to seeing these materials, however?

Meerabelle Jesuthasan, writing for the Pulitzer Center, reports that "teachers across all 50 states have accessed the Pulitzer Center educational resources since the project's launch, and many have shared their students' work by posting to Twitter and emailing [us] student work." Hundreds of schools order class sets of the Times issue in question, as well.

Jesuthasan continues, "Teachers are using the magazine in their classes to teach subjects ranging from English to History and Social Studies, and their engagement with the project has guided students in creating essay, poetry, visual art, performances, and live events that demonstrate their learning."

As an example of this, the school district of Buffalo, New York, included the project as a mandated part of the curriculum for seventh through 12th graders. With what result? Dr. Fatima Morrell, associate superintendent for culturally and linguistically responsive initiatives for Buffalo Public Schools, says this: "One of the things that we are looking at in implementing The 1619 Project is to let everyone know that the issues around the legacy of enslavement that exist today, it's an American issue. it's not a Black issue."

And how are students reacting? One teacher, reporting to the Pulitzer Center, said this: "I think it was really powerful for them [that is, the students]—one, to hear someone's story about how growing up, they felt disenchanted with the idea of America, and two, how Hannah-Jones communicated that black Americans have really improved our country." She reports that, as her students read the opening essay of the project, students' eyes would light up at certain parts and reveal in the prose.

Another teacher reports, talking about her students, "They jumped right in, captivated by the text and images." That same teacher then asked her students to think about why all Americans should know about the things included in the project. One student wrote in an essay, "I think Americans should know about this because this is how unfair their ancestors treated slaves." Another student wrote, "America must know about the beginning of slavery because they used our backs to create what they call now the United States."

What about students in communities that are not predominantly black or white? Walter Diaz, a bilingual Spanish social studies teacher who mainly instructs students from Puerto Rico, had this to say: "Will we just be bystanders, enablers or perpetrators in our BPS Latino students not succeeding or will we be part of the positive change?"

Yes, ultimately, the curriculum is meant to be about America, not black or white America, but the country that exists today. Everyone, or every race or background, is invited to engage with the material to better understand where America comes from and where it is going.

Chapter 7

Ruining, Re-Writing, or Restoring History

As we have seen in this book, The 1619 Project was published to highlight an unsung thread of American history or point out that just about every aspect of our culture, economy, and politics relates in some way to the legacy of enslavement.

And yet, the project took a step further than that. Contributors asked us to re-imagine popular American heroes and patriots, such as Thomas Jefferson and Abraham Lincoln. They posited that the colonists declared their independence in order to preserve their right to own slaves. Moreover, they paint a somewhat depressing picture of modern America as a place in which rights are still crushed under the boot of racism and capitalism, telling its readers that black Americans will have to continue to endure this oppression for a long time to come.

In addition to re-writing history, the project reshapes the present because the past and today are intimately linked.

This is the point Adam Serwer makes in his article for The Atlantic, saying that the core issue in the dispute and defending of The 1619 Project is "a fundamental disagreement over the trajectory of American society."

How does this disagreement start back in our history? How does casting past events in a new light affect our view of the present?

The Past—an Optimistic or Pessimistic View?

Serwer writes, "US history is often taught and popularly understood through the eyes of its great men, who are seen as either heroic or tragic figures in a global struggle for human freedom." Like myths of ancient times, such as Odysseus or Hercules, our modern myths includes George Washington, Thomas Jefferson, Abraham Lincoln, and Martin Luther King Jr. But, when race issues and slavery are put front and center in the discussion, those same "great men" will look very different.

When historians wrote a letter in protest of The 1619 Project, they protected a vision of American history that shows a slow but constant march toward a more perfect union. It is an optimistic view. Those same historians see the project's view of history as much more pessimistic.

"The biggest obstacle to teaching slavery effectively in America is the deep, abiding American need to conceive of and understand our history as 'progress,' as the story of people and a nation that always sought the improvement of mankind, the advancement of liberty and justice, the broadening of the pursuit of happiness for all," David Blight, a Yale historian, wrote.

The question, though, is this: is that optimistic history focused on progress the most realistic view of our history?

David Blight continues, "While there are many real threads to this story—about immigration, about our creeds and ideologies, and about race and emancipation and civil rights, there is also the broad, untidy underside."

In other words, as much as many would like to defend the "glorious" white-washed history because of its pessimism, it simply is not the whole picture. The goal of The 1619 Project is to share that "untidy underside" of American history, perhaps flipping it over and making the underside the part people see first.

1619's Legacy

While some criticized The 1619 Project, saying it was "a displacement of historical understanding by ideology," or a "falsification of history," or even an "extremely dangerous" racialist narrative, the intention and effects of the project never were to re-write or ruin history.

Instead, the contributors of The 1619 Project intended to present a different side to history, a side that is often overlooked, only briefly taught in schools, and quickly swept under the rug.

The core effect of the project has been to foment open and renewed discussions about where our country comes from and where it is going. Those that critique the project are—whether they like it or not—only adding to the conversation and making even more people think about these important matters.

One historian put it this way, "We shall never have a science of history until we have in our colleges men *and women* who regard the truth as more important than the defense of the white race." Yes, while The 1619 Project did go too far in some statements, needing to backtrack and edit their material or add more context to some claims, anyone that is overly vigorous in fighting against the premise of the project must ask him or herself: Am I defending American history or White American history? Am I interested in the pursuit of the truth, no matter how ugly? Am I committed to understanding the past better so we can build a better future?

Then again, critics of the project have struck a strong chord with many when they say that America painted by the project is pessimistic in nature. Does it point out the truth, or does it incite a greater divide between black and white Americans? Where will the conversation go next?

Time, as they say, will tell.

Made in United States
Orlando, FL
12 December 2021

11611945R00040